great
GRILLING

Publications International, Ltd.

Pictured on the front cover: Beer-Brined Grilled Pork Chop *(page 78).*

Pictured on the back cover *(clockwise from top left):* Spicy Grilled Corn *(page 106),* Garlic & Lemon Herb Marinated Chicken *(page 76),* Grilled Salmon with Pineapple Salsa *(page 8)* and Bacon and Blue Cheese Stuffed Burger *(page 44).*

ISBN-13: 978-1-4508-6207-3
ISBN-10: 1-4508-6207-1

Manufactured in China.

8 7 6 5 4 3 2 1

Microwave Cooking: Microwave ovens vary in wattage. Use the cooking times as guidelines and check for doneness before adding more time.

Preparation/Cooking Times: Preparation times are based on the approximate amount of time required to assemble the recipe before cooking, baking, chilling or serving. These times include preparation steps such as measuring, chopping and mixing. The fact that some preparations and cooking can be done simultaneously is taken into account. Preparation of optional ingredients and serving suggestions is not included.

CONTENTS

GRILLING CLASSICS

Sesame-Garlic Flank Steak

- 1 **beef flank steak (about 1¼ pounds)**
- 2 **tablespoons soy sauce**
- 2 **tablespoons hoisin sauce**
- 1 **tablespoon dark sesame oil**
- 2 **cloves garlic, minced**

1 Score steak lightly with sharp knife in diamond pattern on both sides; place in large resealable food storage bag. Combine soy sauce, hoisin sauce, sesame oil and garlic in small bowl; pour over steak. Seal bag; turn to coat. Marinate in refrigerator at least 2 hours or up to 24 hours, turning once.

2 Prepare grill for direct cooking.

3 Drain steak, reserving marinade. Grill steak, covered, over medium heat 13 to 18 minutes until medium rare (145°F) or to desired doneness, turning and brushing with marinade halfway through cooking time. Discard remaining marinade.

4 Remove steak to cutting board; carve across the grain into thin slices.

MAKES 4 SERVINGS

Honey and Mustard Glazed Chicken

1 whole chicken (4 to 5 pounds)
1 tablespoon vegetable oil
¼ cup honey
2 tablespoons Dijon mustard
1 tablespoon reduced-sodium soy sauce
½ teaspoon ground ginger
⅛ teaspoon black pepper
   Dash salt

1 Prepare grill for indirect cooking.

2 Remove giblets from chicken cavity and discard. Pull chicken skin over neck; secure with metal skewer. Tuck wings under back; tie legs together with wet string. Lightly brush chicken with oil.

3 Combine honey, mustard, soy sauce, ginger, pepper and salt in small bowl.

4 Place chicken, breast side up, on grid directly over drip pan. Grill chicken, covered, over medium-high heat 1 hour 30 minutes or until cooked through (165°F). Brush with glaze every 10 minutes during last 30 minutes of cooking time.*

5 Remove chicken to cutting board; cover loosely with foil. Let stand 15 minutes before carving.

MAKES 4 SERVINGS

If using grill with heat on one side (rather than around drip pan), rotate chicken 180 degrees after 45 minutes of cooking time.

GRILLING CLASSICS

Grilled Salmon with Pineapple Salsa

½ **pineapple, cut into ½-inch cubes (about 2 cups)**
½ **cup Mexican beer**
1 **tablespoon sugar**
¼ **cup finely chopped red onion**
¼ **cup finely chopped red bell pepper**
2 **tablespoons chopped fresh cilantro**
1 **tablespoon lime juice**
1 **teaspoon salt, divided**
4 **salmon fillets (6 to 8 ounces each)**
1 **tablespoon olive oil**
¼ **teaspoon black pepper**

1 Combine pineapple, beer and sugar in medium bowl; refrigerate 1 hour. Drain and discard all but 2 tablespoons liquid. Add onion, bell pepper, cilantro, lime juice and ½ teaspoon salt to pineapple mixture; refrigerate 1 hour or overnight.

2 Prepare grill for direct cooking. Oil grid. Rub salmon fillets with oil; sprinkle with remaining ½ teaspoon salt and black pepper.

3 Grill salmon 5 minutes per side over medium-high heat or until fish just begins to flake when tested with fork. Serve with salsa.

MAKES 4 SERVINGS

GRILLING CLASSICS

Buffalo Chicken Drumsticks

8 large chicken drumsticks (about 2 pounds)
3 tablespoons hot pepper sauce
1 tablespoon vegetable oil
1 clove garlic, minced
¼ cup mayonnaise
3 tablespoons sour cream
1 tablespoon white wine vinegar
¼ teaspoon sugar
⅓ cup (about 1½ ounces) crumbled Roquefort or blue cheese
2 cups hickory chips
   Celery sticks

1 Place chicken in large resealable food storage bag. Combine hot pepper sauce, oil and garlic in small bowl; pour over chicken. Seal bag; turn to coat. Marinate in refrigerator at least 1 hour or up to 24 hours for hotter flavor, turning occasionally.

2 For blue cheese dressing, combine mayonnaise, sour cream, vinegar and sugar in another small bowl. Stir in cheese; cover and refrigerate until ready to serve.

3 Prepare grill for direct cooking. Soak hickory chips in cold water 20 minutes. Drain chicken; discard marinade. Drain hickory chips; sprinkle over coals.

4 Grill chicken, covered, over medium-high heat 25 to 30 minutes or until cooked through (165°F), turning occasionally. Serve with blue cheese dressing and celery sticks.

MAKES 4 SERVINGS

Classic California Burgers

2 tablespoons FRENCH'S® Honey Dijon Mustard
2 tablespoons mayonnaise
2 tablespoons sour cream
1 pound ground beef
2 tablespoons FRENCH'S® Worcestershire Sauce
1⅓ cups FRENCH'S® Cheddar or Original French Fried Onions, divided
½ teaspoon garlic salt
¼ teaspoon ground black pepper
4 hamburger rolls, split and toasted
½ small avocado, sliced
½ cup sprouts

1 Combine mustard, mayonnaise and sour cream; set aside.

2 Combine beef, Worcestershire, ⅔ cup French Fried Onions and seasonings. Form into 4 patties. Grill over high heat until juices run clear (160°F internal temperature).

3 Place burgers on rolls. Top each with mustard sauce, avocado slices, sprouts and remaining onions, dividing evenly. Cover with top halves of rolls.

MAKES 4 SERVINGS

BBQ Cheese Burgers: Top each burger with 1 slice American cheese, 1 tablespoon barbecue sauce and 2 tablespoons French Fried Onions.

Pizza Burgers: Top each burger with pizza sauce, mozzarella cheese and French Fried Onions.

Prep Time: 10 minutes
Cook Time: 10 minutes

GRILLING CLASSICS

Blackened Catfish
with Creole Vegetables

⅔ cup CATTLEMEN'S® Authentic Smoke House Barbecue Sauce or
  CATTLEMEN'S® Award Winning Classic Barbecue Sauce
⅓ cup FRANK'S® REDHOT® Original Cayenne Pepper Sauce
2 tablespoons Southwest chile seasoning blend or Cajun seasoning
  blend
1 tablespoon olive oil
4 skinless catfish or sea bass fillets (1½ pounds)
  Salt and pepper to taste
  Creole Vegetables (recipe follows)

1 Combine barbecue sauce, Frank's RedHot Sauce, seasoning blend and oil. Reserve ½ cup mixture for Creole Vegetables.

2 Season fish with salt and pepper to taste. Baste fish with remaining barbecue mixture.

3 Cook fish on a well-greased grill over medium direct heat 5 minutes per side until fish is opaque in center, turning once. Serve with Creole Vegetables.

MAKES 4 SERVINGS

Creole Vegetables

1 red, green or orange bell pepper, cut into quarters
1 large green zucchini or summer squash, cut in half crosswise,
  then lengthwise into thick slices
1 large white onion, sliced ½ inch thick
  Vegetable cooking spray

Arrange vegetables on skewers. Coat vegetables with cooking spray. Grill vegetables over medium direct heat until lightly charred and tender, basting often with reserved ½ cup barbecue sauce mixture.

MAKES 4 SERVINGS

Apricot and Honey Glazed Baby Back Ribs

1 tablespoon garlic powder
1 tablespoon ground cumin
1 teaspoon salt
½ teaspoon black pepper
6 pounds baby back ribs (2 racks), halved
1 bottle (12 ounces) honey wheat lager
1 cup apricot preserves
3 tablespoons honey

1 Prepare grill for indirect cooking. Oil grid.

2 Combine garlic powder, cumin, salt and pepper in small bowl; rub over both sides of ribs.

3 Grill ribs, covered, meat side down, over medium heat 30 minutes. Turn and grill 30 minutes.

4 Meanwhile, combine lager, preserves and honey in medium saucepan over medium-high heat. Bring to a boil; cook 20 minutes or until thick and reduced to ¾ cup.

5 After ribs have cooked 1 hour, turn and brush with half of glaze. Grill 15 minutes; turn and brush with remaining glaze. Grill 15 minutes or until ribs are tender.

MAKES 6 TO 8 SERVINGS

GRILLING CLASSICS

Grilled Fish Tacos

  1 pound skinless mahi mahi, halibut or tilapia fillets
  ¾ teaspoon chili powder
  ½ cup salsa, divided
  2 cups packaged coleslaw mix or shredded cabbage
  ¼ cup sour cream
  4 tablespoons chopped fresh cilantro, divided
  8 (6-inch) corn tortillas, warmed according to package directions

1 Prepare grill for direct cooking.

2 Sprinkle fish with chili powder. Spoon ¼ cup salsa over fish; let stand 10 minutes. Meanwhile, combine coleslaw mix, remaining ¼ cup salsa, sour cream and 2 tablespoons cilantro in large bowl; mix well.

3 Place fish, salsa side up, on grid. Grill fish, covered, over medium heat 8 to 10 minutes until fish is opaque in center. (Do not turn fish.)

4 Slice fish crosswise into thin strips or cut into chunks. Fill warm tortillas with fish and coleslaw mix. Sprinkle with remaining cilantro.

MAKES 4 SERVINGS

GRILLING CLASSICS

Chipotle Spice-Rubbed Beer Can Chicken

2 tablespoons packed brown sugar
2 teaspoons smoked paprika
2 teaspoons ground cumin
1 teaspoon salt
1 teaspoon garlic powder
1 teaspoon chili powder
½ teaspoon ground chipotle pepper
1 whole chicken (3½ to 4 pounds), rinsed and patted dry
1 can (12 ounces) beer

1 Prepare grill for indirect cooking. Oil grid.

2 Combine brown sugar, paprika, cumin, salt, garlic powder, chili powder and chipotle pepper in small bowl. Gently loosen skin of chicken over breast, legs and thighs. Rub sugar mixture under and over skin and inside cavity. Discard one fourth of beer. Hold chicken upright with cavity pointing down; insert beer can into cavity.

3 Place chicken on grid, standing upright on can; spread legs slightly for support. Grill chicken, covered, over medium heat 1 hour 15 minutes or until cooked through (165°F).

4 Lift chicken off beer can using metal tongs. Let stand upright on cutting board 5 minutes before carving.

MAKES 4 SERVINGS

Grilled Tuna Salad
with Avocado Dressing

- 1 packet (1.25 ounces) ORTEGA® Taco Seasoning Mix
- ½ cup water
- 1½ pounds tuna steaks
- 1 ripe avocado
- ¼ cup ORTEGA® Salsa, any variety
- ¼ cup sour cream
- Juice of ½ lime
- ½ teaspoon POLANER® Chopped Garlic
- ½ teaspoon salt
- 2 heads romaine lettuce, chopped
- Salt and black pepper, to taste

COMBINE seasoning mix and water in shallow pan. Place tuna steaks in pan. Turn over to coat well. Marinate, covered, 15 minutes in refrigerator. Turn tuna steaks over again and marinate in refrigerator 15 minutes longer.

PREHEAT grill until piping hot, about 15 minutes. Grill tuna steaks 4 minutes on each side (fish will be pink on inside). Grill longer for well-done fish, if desired.

FOR Avocado Dressing, slice and pit avocado; scrape avocado flesh into small bowl. Add salsa, sour cream, lime juice, garlic and salt. Mix with fork, mashing avocado to combine ingredients well. Toss with chopped lettuce. Divide mixture among serving plates.

SLICE tuna steaks into strips and place on lettuce. Add salt and pepper, to taste.

MAKES 6 SERVINGS

Note: Avocado Dressing can also be served with taco chips as Avocado-Salsa Dip. For taco chips, preheat oven to 350°F. Place ORTEGA® Yellow Corn Taco Shells on baking sheet and bake 10 minutes. Remove from oven and gently break into pieces. Sprinkle with salt, if desired. Serve with dip.

Chicken and Vegetable Satay with Peanut Sauce

1½ pounds boneless skinless chicken thighs, cut into 32 (1½-inch) cubes
⅔ cup Thai or other Asian beer, divided
3 tablespoons packed dark brown sugar, divided
1 tablespoon plus 2 teaspoons lime juice, divided
3 cloves garlic, minced, divided
1¼ teaspoons curry powder, divided
½ cup coconut milk
½ cup chunky peanut butter
1 tablespoon fish sauce
3 tablespoons peanut oil, divided
¼ cup finely chopped onion
24 medium mushrooms, stems trimmed
4 green onions, cut into 24 (1-inch) pieces

1 Place chicken in large resealable food storage bag. Combine ⅓ cup beer, 1 tablespoon brown sugar, 1 tablespoon lime juice, 2 cloves garlic and 1 teaspoon curry powder in small bowl; pour over chicken. Seal bag; turn to coat. Marinate in refrigerator 2 hours, turning occasionally.

2 Meanwhile, combine remaining ⅓ cup beer, 2 tablespoons sugar, 2 teaspoons lime juice, coconut milk, peanut butter and fish sauce in medium bowl. Heat 1 tablespoon oil in small saucepan over medium-high heat. Add onion and remaining clove garlic; cook 3 minutes or until just beginning to soften. Add remaining ¼ teaspoon curry powder; cook 15 seconds. Stir in coconut milk mixture. Reduce heat to medium and simmer about 15 minutes or until thickened, stirring often. Keep warm.

3 Prepare grill for direct cooking. Oil grid. Remove chicken from marinade; discard marinade. Alternately thread chicken, mushrooms and green onions onto 8 skewers. Brush with remaining 2 tablespoons oil. Grill 8 to 10 minutes over medium-high heat, turning occasionally, until chicken is cooked through and mushrooms are tender. Serve with peanut sauce.

MAKES 4 SERVINGS

Marinated Italian Sausage and Peppers

    4 hot or sweet Italian sausage links
    1 large onion, cut into rings
    1 large bell pepper, cut into quarters
    ½ cup olive oil
    ¼ cup red wine vinegar
    2 tablespoons chopped fresh parsley
    1 tablespoon dried oregano
    2 cloves garlic, crushed
    1 teaspoon salt
    1 teaspoon black pepper
    Horseradish-Mustard Spread (recipe follows)

1 Place sausage, onion and bell pepper in large resealable food storage bag. Combine oil, vinegar, parsley, oregano, garlic, salt and black pepper in small bowl; pour over sausage and vegetables. Seal bag; turn to coat. Marinate in refrigerator 1 to 2 hours.

2 Prepare Horseradish-Mustard Spread; set aside. Prepare grill for direct cooking. Oil grid.

3 Drain sausage, onion and bell pepper; reserve marinade. Grill sausage, covered, over medium heat 5 minutes. Turn sausage and place onion and bell pepper on grid; brush with reserved marinade. Discard remaining marinade. Grill, covered, 5 minutes or until sausage is cooked through and vegetables are crisp-tender. Serve with Horseradish-Mustard Spread.

MAKES 4 SERVINGS

Horseradish-Mustard Spread: Combine 3 tablespoons mayonnaise, 1 tablespoon prepared horseradish, 1 tablespoon Dijon mustard, 1 tablespoon chopped fresh parsley, 2 teaspoons garlic powder and 1 teaspoon black pepper in small bowl; mix well.

GRILLING CLASSICS

Mixed Grill Kabobs

　1 **pound boneless beef sirloin, cut into 1-inch cubes**
　2 **large red, orange or yellow bell peppers, cut into chunks**
12 **strips bacon, blanched***
12 **ounces smoked sausage or kielbasa, cut into ½-inch slices**
　1 **cup peeled red pearl onions or red onion chunks**
　1 **pound pork tenderloin, cut lengthwise in half; then into ¼-inch wide long strips**
　1 **cup pineapple wedges**
1½ **cups CATTLEMEN'S® Award Winning Classic Barbecue Sauce**

*To blanch bacon, place bacon strips into boiling water for 1 minute. Drain thoroughly.

1 Arrange beef cubes and 1 bell pepper on metal skewers, weaving bacon strips around all. Place sausage, 1 pepper and onions on separate skewers. Weave strips of pork on additional skewers with pineapple wedges.

2 Baste kabobs with some of the barbecue sauce. Cook on a well-greased grill over medium-high direct heat 10 to 15 minutes, basting often with remaining barbecue sauce.

3 Serve trio of kabobs to each person with additional sauce.

MAKES 6 TO 8 SERVINGS

Tip: To easily cut pork, freeze about 30 minutes until very firm.

Note: You may substitute Cattlemen's® Authentic Smoke House or Golden Honey Barbecue Sauce.

Prep Time: 20 minutes
Cook Time: 10 to 15 minutes

GRILLING CLASSICS

BURGER PARTY

Chutney Turkey Burgers

  1 pound ground turkey
  ½ cup prepared chutney, divided
  ½ teaspoon salt
  ½ teaspoon pepper
  ⅛ teaspoon hot pepper sauce
  ½ cup nonfat plain yogurt
  1 teaspoon curry powder
  4 hamburger buns, split

1 Preheat grill for direct-heat cooking.

2 In medium bowl, combine turkey, ¼ cup chutney, salt, pepper and hot pepper sauce. Shape turkey mixture into 4 burgers, approximately 3½ inches in diameter. Grill turkey burgers 5 to 6 minutes per side until 165°F is reached on meat thermometer and turkey is no longer pink in center.

3 In small bowl, combine yogurt, curry powder and remaining ¼ cup chutney.

4 To serve, place burgers on bottom halves of buns; spoon yogurt mixture over burgers and cover with top halves of buns.

MAKES 4 SERVINGS

Favorite recipe from
National Turkey
Federation

Greek Lamb Burgers

¼ cup pine nuts
1 pound ground lamb
¼ cup finely chopped yellow onion
3 cloves garlic, minced, divided
¾ teaspoon salt
¼ teaspoon black pepper
¼ cup plain yogurt
¼ teaspoon sugar
4 slices red onion (¼ inch thick)
1 tablespoon olive oil
8 pumpernickel bread slices
12 thin cucumber slices
4 tomato slices

1 Prepare grill for direct cooking. Spread pine nuts in small skillet. Cook over medium heat 1 to 2 minutes or until nuts are lightly browned, stirring frequently.

2 Combine lamb, pine nuts, yellow onion, 2 cloves garlic, salt and pepper in large bowl; mix well. Shape into 4 patties about 4 inches in diameter and ½ inch thick. Combine yogurt, sugar and remaining 1 clove garlic in small bowl; set aside.

3 Brush one side of patties and red onion slices with oil; place on grid, oiled sides down. Brush tops with oil. Grill patties, covered, over medium-high heat 4 to 5 minutes per side until medium (160°F) or to desired doneness. Grill bread 1 to 2 minutes per side during last few minutes of grilling.

4 Top 4 bread slices with burgers, red onion, cucumber and tomato. Top with yogurt mixture and remaining 4 bread slices.

MAKES 4 SERVINGS

Western Barbecue Burgers with Beer Barbecue Sauce

1½ **pounds ground beef**
  1 **cup smokehouse-style barbecue sauce**
¼ **cup brown ale**
½ **teaspoon salt**
¼ **teaspoon black pepper**
  1 **red onion, cut into ½-inch-thick slices**
  4 **hamburger buns**
  8 **slices thick-cut bacon, crisp-cooked**
    Lettuce leaves
    Tomato slices

1 Prepare grill for direct cooking.

2 Shape beef into 4 patties about ¾ inch thick.

3 Combine barbecue sauce, ale, salt and pepper in small saucepan. Bring to a boil; boil 1 minute. Set aside.

4 Grill patties, covered, over medium-high heat 4 to 5 minutes per side until medium (160°F) or to desired doneness. Grill onion 4 minutes or until softened and slightly charred, turning occasionally.

5 Serve burgers on buns topped with onion, bacon, barbecue sauce mixture, lettuce and tomatoes.

MAKES 4 SERVINGS

BURGER PARTY

Aloha Burgers with Pineapple Chutney

2 tablespoons butter
2 tablespoons packed dark brown sugar
¼ cup cola
¼ cup balsamic vinegar
½ medium red onion, diced
1 small tomato, seeded and diced
1½ cups diced pineapple
2 pounds ground beef
2 tablespoons teriyaki sauce
2 teaspoons Worcestershire sauce
2 teaspoons onion powder
2 teaspoons black pepper
1½ teaspoons salt
Additional salt and black pepper
6 brioche rolls or hamburger buns, toasted

1 Melt butter in medium saucepan over medium-low heat; stir in brown sugar until blended. Stir in cola and vinegar; bring to a boil. Reduce heat to low; simmer 20 minutes, stirring frequently.

2 Stir in onion; cook and stir 2 minutes over medium heat. Stir in tomato and pineapple; remove from heat.

3 Combine beef, teriyaki sauce, Worcestershire sauce, onion powder, 2 teaspoons pepper and 1½ teaspoons salt in medium bowl; mix lightly. Shape into 6 patties.

4 Prepare grill for direct cooking. Grill patties, covered, over medium-high heat 4 to 5 minutes per side until medium (160°F) or to desired doneness. When cooked to desired doneness, keep warm. Return pineapple mixture to high heat 1 minute; season with salt and pepper. Serve burgers on buns with pineapple chutney.

MAKES 6 SERVINGS

BURGER PARTY

Brie Burgers with Sun-Dried Tomato and Artichoke Spread

1 cup canned quartered artichokes, drained and chopped
½ cup oil-packed sun-dried tomatoes, drained and chopped, divided
2 tablespoons mayonnaise
1 tablespoon plus 1 teaspoon minced garlic, divided
1 teaspoon black pepper, divided
½ teaspoon salt, divided
1½ pounds ground beef
¼ cup chopped shallots
¼ pound Brie cheese, sliced
2 tablespoons butter, softened
4 egg or Kaiser rolls, split
Heirloom tomato slices
Arugula or lettuce leaves

1 Prepare grill for direct cooking.

2 Combine artichokes, ¼ cup sun-dried tomatoes, mayonnaise, 1 teaspoon garlic, ½ teaspoon pepper and ¼ teaspoon salt in small bowl; mix well.

3 Combine beef, shallots, remaining ¼ cup sun-dried tomatoes, 1 tablespoon garlic, ½ teaspoon pepper and ¼ teaspoon salt in large bowl; mix lightly. Shape into 4 patties.

4 Grill patties, covered, over medium heat 4 to 5 minutes per side until medium (160°F) or to desired doneness. Top each burger with cheese during last 2 minutes of grilling.

5 Spread butter on cut surfaces of rolls; grill or toast until lightly browned. Spread artichoke mixture on bottom halves of rolls. Top with tomato slices, burgers, arugula and top halves of rolls.

MAKES 4 SERVINGS

BURGER PARTY

Turkey Burgers with Pesto-Red Pepper Mayonnaise

¼ cup HELLMANN'S® or BEST FOODS® Light Mayonnaise*
1 tablespoon prepared pesto
1 tablespoon finely chopped roasted red pepper
4 turkey burgers
4 Kaiser or whole grain rolls
   Tomato slices
   Lettuce leaves
   Onion slices (optional)

*Also terrific with HELLMANN'S® or BEST FOODS® Low Fat Mayonnaise Dressing or Canola Cholesterol Free Mayonnaise.

Combine HELLMANN'S® or BEST FOODS® Light Mayonnaise, pesto and roasted pepper in small bowl; set aside.

Grill or broil turkey burgers 8 minutes or until thoroughly cooked, turning once. To serve, evenly spread Mayonnaise mixture on rolls, then top with burgers, tomato, lettuce, onion and dollop of Mayonnaise mixture.

MAKES 4 SERVINGS

Tip: To perk up the flavor of your burgers, mix WISH-BONE® Italian Dressing into the ground beef or ground turkey.

Prep Time: 10 minutes
Cook Time: 8 minutes

BURGER PARTY

Gourmet Burgers with Pancetta and Gorgonzola

1½ **pounds ground beef**

4 **ounces (about ½ cup) gorgonzola or blue cheese crumbles**

2 **tablespoons mayonnaise**

1 **red bell pepper, quartered**

4 **thick slices red onion**

  Salt and black pepper

  Oak leaf or baby romaine lettuce

4 **to 8 slices pancetta or bacon, crisp-cooked**

4 **egg or brioche rolls, split and toasted**

1 Prepare grill for direct cooking.

2 Shape beef into 4 patties about ¾ inch thick. Combine cheese and mayonnaise in small bowl; refrigerate until ready to serve.

3 Grill bell pepper and onion, covered, over medium-high heat 8 to 10 minutes or until browned, turning once. (Use grill basket, if desired.) Transfer to plate; keep warm.

4 Grill patties, covered, over medium heat 4 to 5 minutes per side until medium (160°F) or to desired doneness. Season with salt and black pepper.

5 Spread cheese mixture on cut surfaces of rolls. Top bottom halves of rolls with lettuce, burgers, pancetta, onion, bell pepper and top halves of rolls.

MAKES 4 SERVINGS

Bacon and Blue Cheese Stuffed Burgers

4 slices applewood-smoked bacon or regular bacon
1 small red onion, finely chopped
2 tablespoons crumbled blue cheese
1 tablespoon butter, softened
1½ pounds ground beef
   Salt and black pepper
4 onion or plain hamburger rolls
   Lettuce leaves

1 Cook bacon in large skillet over medium-high heat until chewy. Drain on paper towels. Add onion to same skillet; cook and stir until soft. Cool slightly.

2 Finely chop bacon. Combine bacon, onion, blue cheese and butter in small bowl; mix well. Prepare grill for direct cooking.

3 Shape beef into 8 into thin patties about 4 inches in diameter. Season with salt and pepper. Place 2 tablespoons bacon mixture in center of each of 4 patties; cover with remaining patties and pinch edges together to seal.

4 Grill patties, covered, over medium-high heat 4 to 5 minutes per side until medium (160°F) or to desired doneness. Serve burgers on rolls with lettuce.

MAKES 4 SERVINGS

Tip: If you want juicy, flavorful burgers, do not flatten patties while cooking. Pressing down on the patties with a spatula not only squeezes out tasty juices, but in this recipe it might also cause the stuffing to pop out.

Deluxe Bacon and Gouda Burgers

1½ **pounds ground beef**
⅓ **cup mayonnaise**
1 **teaspoon minced garlic**
¼ **teaspoon Dijon mustard**
2 **thick slices red onion**
   Salt and black pepper
4 to 8 **slices Gouda cheese**
   Butter lettuce leaves
4 **onion rolls, split and toasted**
   Tomato slices
4 to 8 **slices bacon, crisp-cooked**

1 Prepare grill for direct cooking.

2 Shape beef into 4 patties about ¾ inch thick. Combine mayonnaise, garlic and mustard in small bowl; mix well.

3 Grill patties and onion slices, covered, over medium heat 4 to 5 minutes per side until medium (160°F) or to desired doneness. Remove onion when slightly browned. Season burgers with salt and pepper. Top with cheese during last 2 minutes of grilling.

4 Place lettuce on bottom halves of rolls; top with mayonnaise mixture, burgers, onion, tomato, bacon and top halves of rolls.

MAKES 4 SERVINGS

Southwest Pesto Burgers

½ cup fresh cilantro, stemmed
1½ teaspoons chopped jalapeño pepper
1 clove garlic
¾ teaspoon salt, divided
¼ cup vegetable oil
2 tablespoons mayonnaise
1¼ pounds ground beef
4 slices pepper jack cheese
4 Kaiser rolls, split
1 ripe avocado, sliced
Salsa

Jalapeño peppers can sting and irritate the skin, so wear rubber gloves when handling peppers and do not touch your eyes.

1 For pesto, combine cilantro, jalapeño, garlic and ¼ teaspoon salt in food processor; process until garlic is minced. With motor running, slowly add oil through feed tube; process until thick paste forms. Combine mayonnaise and 1 tablespoon pesto in small bowl; mix well.

2 Prepare grill for direct cooking.

3 Combine beef, remaining ¼ cup pesto and ½ teaspoon salt in large bowl; mix lightly. Shape into 4 patties.

4 Grill patties, covered, over medium heat 4 to 5 minutes per side until medium (160°F) or to desired doneness. Top each burger with cheese during last minute of grilling.

5 Place burgers on bottom halves of rolls. Top with mayonnaise mixture, avocado, salsa and top halves of rolls.

MAKES 4 SERVINGS

Backyard Barbecue Burgers

1½ **pounds ground beef**
⅓ **cup barbecue sauce, divided**
1 **onion, cut into thick slices**
1 to 2 **tomatoes, sliced**
1 to 2 **tablespoons olive oil**
6 **Kaiser rolls, split**
6 **leaves green or red leaf lettuce**

1 Prepare grill for direct cooking.

2 Combine beef and 2 tablespoons barbecue sauce in large bowl; mix lightly. Shape into 6 patties about 1 inch thick.

3 Grill patties, covered, over medium heat 4 to 5 minutes per side until medium (160°F) or to desired doneness. Brush both sides with remaining barbecue sauce during last 5 minutes of grilling.

4 Meanwhile, brush onion and tomato slices with oil. Grill onion slices about 10 minutes and tomato slices 2 to 3 minutes.

5 Grill rolls, cut side down, until lightly toasted. Serve burgers on rolls with tomato, onion and lettuce.

MAKES 6 SERVINGS

Wild West Picante Burgers

1 pound ground beef
½ cup PACE® Picante Sauce
4 PEPPERIDGE FARM® Classic Hamburger Buns, split

1 Thoroughly mix the beef and picante sauce in a medium bowl. Shape the mixture into 4 (½-inch thick) burgers.

2 Lightly oil the grill rack and heat the grill to medium. Grill the burgers for 10 minutes or until desired doneness, turning them over halfway through grilling and brushing often with additional picante sauce.

3 Serve the burgers on the buns with additional picante sauce.

MAKES 4 BURGERS

Serving Suggestion: Serve with coleslaw or fresh vegetables and ranch dressing for dipping and corn-on-the cob. For dessert, serve sliced watermelon or fresh fruit salad.

Prep Time: 10 minutes
Cook Time: 10 minutes

Great Grilled Burgers with Spinach Pesto

        Spinach Pesto (recipe follows)
 1½ **pounds ground beef**
  ¼ **teaspoon salt**
  ¼ **teaspoon black pepper**
   4 **to 8 slices provolone cheese**
   4 **crusty Italian rolls, split and toasted**
   4 **to 8 slices tomatoes**
        Oak leaf lettuce

1 Prepare Spinach Pesto. Prepare grill for direct cooking.

2 Combine beef, ¼ cup pesto, salt and pepper in large bowl; mix lightly. Shape into 4 patties about ¾ inch thick.

3 Grill patties, covered, over medium heat 4 to 5 minutes per side until medium (160°F) or to desired doneness. Top each burger with cheese during last 2 minutes of grilling.

4 Spread remaining pesto on cut surfaces of rolls. Top bottom halves of rolls with burgers, tomato, lettuce and top halves of rolls.

MAKES 4 SERVINGS

Spinach Pesto: Combine 2 cups spinach leaves, 3 tablespoons grated Romano cheese, 3 tablespoons olive oil, 1 tablespoon dried basil, 1 tablespoon lemon juice and 3 cloves garlic in food processor or blender; process until smooth. Makes about ½ cup.

BURGER PARTY

HOT & HEARTY

Ginger-Lime Chicken Thighs

 6 boneless skinless chicken thighs
⅓ cup vegetable oil
 3 tablespoons lime juice
 3 tablespoons honey
 2 teaspoons grated fresh ginger *or* 1 teaspoon ground ginger
¼ to ½ teaspoon red pepper flakes

1 Place chicken in large resealable food storage bag. Combine oil, lime juice, honey, ginger and red pepper flakes in small bowl; pour ½ cup marinade over chicken. Seal bag; turn to coat. Marinate in refrigerator 30 to 60 minutes, turning occasionally. Refrigerate remaining marinade.

2 Prepare grill for direct cooking. Oil grid.

3 Remove chicken from marinade; discard marinade. Grill chicken over medium-high heat 12 minutes or until chicken is cooked through, turning once. Brush with reserved marinade during last 5 minutes of cooking.

MAKES 2 TO 4 SERVINGS

Grilled Strip Steaks with Chimichurri

Chimichurri (recipe follows)
4 bone-in strip steaks (8 ounces each), about 1 inch thick
¾ teaspoon salt
¾ teaspoon ground cumin
¼ teaspoon black pepper

1 Prepare Chimichurri. Prepare grill for direct cooking. Oil grid. Sprinkle both sides of steaks with salt, cumin and pepper.

2 Grill steaks, covered, over medium-high heat 8 to 10 minutes until medium rare or to desired doneness, turning once. Serve with Chimichurri.

MAKES 4 SERVINGS

Chimichurri

½ cup packed fresh basil leaves
⅓ cup extra virgin olive oil
¼ cup packed fresh parsley
2 tablespoons packed fresh cilantro
2 tablespoons lemon juice
1 clove garlic
½ teaspoon salt
½ teaspoon grated orange peel
¼ teaspoon ground coriander
⅛ teaspoon black pepper

Combine all ingredients in food processor or blender; process until well blended.

MAKES ABOUT 1 CUP

Mojo Pork with Orange-Apple Salsa

  1 tablespoon minced garlic
  2 tablespoons olive oil
  ½ cup FRANK'S® REDHOT® Original Cayenne Pepper Sauce
  ½ cup orange juice
  2 tablespoons grated orange zest
  ¼ cup minced fresh cilantro
  2 tablespoons chili powder
  1 teaspoon dried oregano
  2 boneless pork tenderloins (2 pounds)
  ½ cup sour cream
    Orange-Apple Salsa (recipe follows)

1 Sauté garlic in oil; cool. Slowly stir in Frank's RedHot Sauce, orange juice, zest, cilantro, chili powder and oregano. Reserve ¼ cup marinade.

2 Place pork into resealable plastic food storage bags. Pour remaining marinade over pork. Seal bags; marinate in refrigerator 1 to 3 hours. Combine remaining marinade with sour cream; set aside in refrigerator.

3 Grill pork over medium-high direct heat for 30 minutes or until center is no longer pink. Slice pork and drizzle with spicy sour cream. Serve with Orange-Apple Salsa.

MAKES 6 TO 8 SERVINGS

Orange-Apple Salsa

  3 navel oranges, peeled, sectioned and cut into small pieces
  2 large apples, cored and diced
  2 tablespoons chopped red onion
  2 tablespoons chopped fresh cilantro
  2 tablespoons FRANK'S® REDHOT® Original Cayenne Pepper Sauce

Combine ingredients in bowl; chill until ready to serve.

MAKES ABOUT 3 CUPS

HOT & HEARTY

Mesquite-Grilled Turkey

2 cups mesquite chips, divided
1 fresh or thawed frozen turkey (10 to 12 pounds)
1 small sweet or Spanish onion, peeled and quartered
1 lemon, quartered
3 fresh tarragon sprigs
1 metal skewer (6 inches long)
2 tablespoons butter, softened
    Salt and pepper
¼ cup (½ stick) butter, melted
2 tablespoons fresh lemon juice
2 tablespoons chopped fresh tarragon *or* 2 teaspoons dried tarragon
2 cloves garlic, minced

1 Soak mesquite chips in cold water 20 minutes. Prepare grill for indirect cooking. Rinse turkey; pat dry with paper towels. Place onion, lemon and tarragon sprigs in cavity. Pull skin over neck; secure with metal skewer. Tuck wing tips under back; tie legs together with wet kitchen string.

2 Spread softened butter over turkey skin; sprinkle with salt and pepper. Insert meat thermometer into center of thickest part of thigh, not touching bone.

3 Drain mesquite chips; sprinkle 1 cup over coals. Place turkey, breast side up, on grid directly over drip pan. Grill turkey, covered, over medium heat 11 to 14 minutes per pound, adding 4 to 9 briquets to both sides of fire each hour to maintain medium coals and adding remaining 1 cup mesquite chips after 1 hour of grilling.

4 Combine melted butter, lemon juice, chopped tarragon and garlic in small bowl. Brush half of mixture over turkey during last 30 minutes of grilling. Brush with remaining butter mixture during last 10 minutes of grilling; grill until cooked through (165°F).

5 Remove turkey to cutting board; cover loosely with foil. Let stand 15 minutes before carving. Discard onion, lemon and tarragon sprigs from cavity.

MAKES 8 TO 10 SERVINGS

HOT & HEARTY

Korean-Style Skirt Steak

1 **pound skirt steak, cut into 4 pieces and pounded to ¼-inch thickness**
½ **cup sliced green onions**
⅓ **cup soy sauce**
¼ **cup unseasoned rice wine vinegar**
2 **tablespoons packed brown sugar**
1 **tablespoon dark sesame oil**
1 **clove garlic, minced**
1 **teaspoon grated ginger**
½ **teaspoon red pepper flakes**
1 **tablespoon sesame seeds**

1 Place steaks in large resealable food storage bag. Combine green onions, soy sauce, vinegar, brown sugar, sesame oil, garlic, ginger and red pepper flakes in medium bowl. Reserve ⅓ cup marinade; pour remaining marinade over steaks. Seal bag; turn to coat. Marinate in refrigerator 20 minutes or up to 4 hours.

2 Prepare grill for direct cooking.

3 Remove steaks from marinade; discard marinade. Grill steaks, covered, over medium heat 4 to 6 minutes or until medium rare, turning once.

4 Remove steaks to cutting board; cover loosely with foil. Let stand 5 minutes before slicing thinly across the grain. Serve with reserved marinade; sprinkle with sesame seeds.

MAKES 4 SERVINGS

HOT & HEARTY

Grilled Vietnamese-Style Chicken Wings

    3 pounds chicken wings
    ⅓ cup honey
    ¼ to ½ cup sliced lemongrass
    ¼ cup fish sauce
    2 tablespoons chopped garlic
    2 tablespoons chopped shallots
    2 tablespoons chopped fresh ginger
    2 tablespoons lime juice
    2 tablespoons canola oil
       Chopped cilantro (optional)

1 Remove and discard wing tips. Cut each wing in half at joint. Place wings in large resealable food storage bag.

2 Combine honey, lemongrass, fish sauce, garlic, shallots, ginger, lime juice and oil in food processor; process until smooth. Pour over wings. Seal bag; turn to coat. Marinate in refrigerator 4 hours or overnight.

3 Prepare grill for direct cooking. Oil grid. Preheat oven to 350°F.

4 Remove wings from marinade; reserve marinade. Grill wings over medium heat 10 minutes or until browned, turning and basting occasionally with marinade. Discard any remaining marinade.

5 Arrange wings in single layer on baking sheet. Bake 20 minutes or until cooked through. Sprinkle with cilantro, if desired.

MAKES 6 TO 8 SERVINGS

HOT & HEARTY

Chipotle-Marinated Beef Flank Steak

1 beef flank steak (about 1½ to 2 pounds) or beef top round steak,
 cut 1 inch thick (about 1¾ pounds)
 Salt

MARINADE
 ⅓ cup fresh lime juice
 ¼ cup chopped fresh cilantro
 1 tablespoon packed brown sugar
 2 teaspoons minced chipotle chilies in adobo sauce
 2 tablespoons adobo sauce (from chilies)
 2 cloves garlic, minced
 1 teaspoon freshly grated lime peel

1 Combine marinade ingredients in small bowl; mix well. Place beef steak and marinade in food-safe plastic bag; turn steak to coat. Close bag securely and marinate in refrigerator 6 hours or as long as overnight.

2 Remove steak from marinade; discard marinade. Place steak on grid over medium, ash-covered coals. Grill flank steak, uncovered, 17 to 21 minutes for medium rare (145°F) to medium (160°F) doneness (top round steak 16 to 18 minutes for medium rare doneness; do not overcook), turning occasionally. Carve steak across the grain into thin slices. Season with salt, as desired.

MAKES 4 TO 6 SERVINGS

Cook's Tip: To broil, place steak on rack in broiler pan so surface of beef is 2 to 3 inches from heat. Broil flank steak 13 to 18 minutes for medium rare to medium doneness (top round steak 17 to 18 minutes for medium rare doneness; do not overcook), turning once.

Cook's Tip: To prepare on gas grill, preheat grill according to manufacturer's directions for medium heat. Grill flank steak, covered, 16 to 21 minutes for medium rare (145°F) to medium (160°F) doneness (top round steak 16 to 19 minutes for medium rare doneness; do not overcook), turning occasionally.

Prep and Cook Time: 30 minutes
Marinate Time: 6 hours or overnight

Favorite recipe Courtesy The Beef Checkoff

HOT & HEARTY

Chicken with Grilled Pineapple Salsa

1¼ cups WISH-BONE® Italian Dressing or Robusto Italian Dressing
¼ cup firmly packed dark brown sugar
¼ cup plus 2 tablespoons chopped fresh cilantro
2 pounds chicken thighs
2 tablespoons orange juice
¼ teaspoon salt
⅛ teaspoon ground red pepper
1 medium pineapple, peeled and cut into ¾-inch-thick slices
1 large red onion, cut into ½-inch-thick slices

1 Blend Wish-Bone Italian Dressing, sugar and ¼ cup cilantro for marinade. Pour ¾ cup marinade over chicken in large, shallow nonaluminum baking dish or plastic bag; turn to coat. Cover, or close bag, and marinate in refrigerator, turning occasionally, 3 to 24 hours. Refrigerate remaining marinade.

2 Combine 2 tablespoons refrigerated marinade, remaining 2 tablespoons cilantro, orange juice, salt and pepper in medium bowl for salsa; set aside.

3 Remove chicken from marinade, discarding marinade. Grill or broil chicken, pineapple and onion, turning once and brushing frequently with remaining refrigerated marinade. Grill until pineapple and onion are tender and chicken is thoroughly cooked. Chop pineapple and onion and toss with salsa mixture. Serve salsa with chicken.

MAKES 4 SERVINGS

Prep Time: 10 minutes
Marinate Time: 3 hours
Cook Time: 30 minutes

HOT & HEARTY

Carne Asada

½ cup tequila
¼ cup lime juice
¼ cup lemon juice
¼ cup orange juice
1 medium onion, chopped
½ teaspoon garlic powder
2 teaspoons ORTEGA® Taco Sauce, Hot
1 teaspoon black pepper
2 pounds skirt steak
12 (8-inch) ORTEGA® Flour Soft Tortillas
1 cup ORTEGA® Salsa, any variety
1 cup ORTEGA® Guacamole Style Dip

MIX tequila, juices, onion, garlic powder, taco sauce and pepper in large bowl. Add steak, and turn to coat both sides. Cover and refrigerate 6 to 8 hours, turning steak over occasionally to marinate evenly.

PREHEAT grill. Sprinkle a few drops of water on each tortilla, stack and wrap in aluminum foil. Place on grill to warm.

REMOVE meat from marinade, reserving marinade. Place on grill. Brush steak with marinade. Cook 12 to 15 minutes for medium-rare (or cook until desired doneness); turn steak and tortillas once during cooking. Remove tortillas from grill. Discard remaining marinade.

TRANSFER steak to cutting board. Cut into thin slices. Serve with tortillas, salsa and guacamole.

MAKES 8 SERVINGS

Tip: For additional smoky flavor, try grilling the tortillas before serving them with carne asada.

HOT & HEARTY

Bold and Zesty Beef Back Ribs

    5 pounds beef back ribs, cut into 3- or 4-rib pieces
       Salt and black pepper
    1 teaspoon vegetable oil
    1 small onion, minced
    2 cloves garlic, minced
    1 cup ketchup
    ½ cup chili sauce
    2 tablespoons lemon juice
    1 tablespoon packed brown sugar
    1 teaspoon hot pepper sauce

1 Place ribs in shallow pan; season with salt and pepper. Refrigerate until ready to grill.

2 Prepare grill for indirect cooking.

3 Meanwhile, for barbecue sauce, heat oil in large saucepan over medium heat. Add onion and garlic; cook and stir 5 minutes or until onion is tender. Stir in ketchup, chili sauce, lemon juice, brown sugar and hot pepper sauce. Reduce heat to medium-low; cook 15 minutes, stirring occasionally.

4 Place ribs on grid directly over drip pan; baste generously with sauce. Grill ribs, covered, 45 to 60 minutes or until ribs are tender and browned, turning occasionally.

5 Bring remaining sauce to a boil over medium-high heat; boil 1 minute. Serve ribs with sauce.

MAKES 5 TO 6 SERVINGS

HOT & HEARTY

Garlic & Lemon Herb Marinated Chicken

3 to 4 pounds bone-in chicken pieces, skinned if desired
⅓ cup FRENCH'S® Honey Dijon Mustard
⅓ cup lemon juice
⅓ cup olive oil
3 cloves garlic, minced
1 tablespoon grated lemon zest
1 tablespoon minced fresh thyme or rosemary
1 teaspoon coarse salt
½ teaspoon coarse black pepper

1 Place chicken into resealable plastic food storage bag. Combine remaining ingredients. Pour over chicken. Marinate in refrigerator 1 to 3 hours.

2 Remove chicken from marinade. Grill chicken over medium direct heat for 35 to 45 minutes until juices run clear near bone (170°F for breast meat; 180°F for dark meat). Serve with additional mustard on the side.

MAKES 4 SERVINGS

Tip: This marinade is also great on whole chicken or pork chops.

Prep Time: 10 minutes
Marinate Time: 1 hour
Cook Time: 45 minutes

HOT & HEARTY

Beer-Brined Grilled Pork Chops

1 bottle (12 ounces) dark beer
¼ cup dark brown sugar
1 tablespoon salt
1 tablespoon chili powder
2 cloves garlic, minced
3 cups ice water
4 pork chops (1 inch thick)

1 Whisk beer, brown sugar, salt, chili powder and garlic in medium bowl until salt is dissolved. Add ice water and stir until ice melts. Add pork chops; place plate on top to keep chops submerged in brine. Refrigerate 3 to 4 hours.

2 Prepare grill for direct cooking.

3 Drain pork chops; pat dry with paper towels. Grill pork, covered, over medium heat 10 to 12 minutes or until barely pink in center.

MAKES 4 SERVINGS

Tip: Brining adds flavor and moisture to meats. Be sure that your pork chops have not been injected with a sodium solution (check the package label) or they could end up too salty.

HOT & HEARTY

Steak and Mushroom Skewers

¼ cup Italian salad dressing

2 tablespoons Worcestershire sauce

¾ pound beef top sirloin steak, cut into 24 (1-inch) cubes

24 medium whole mushrooms (about 12 ounces)

¼ cup mayonnaise

¼ cup sour cream

1 clove garlic, minced

¼ to ½ teaspoon dried rosemary

¼ teaspoon salt

1 medium zucchini, cut into 24 (1-inch) pieces

1 medium green bell pepper, cut into 24 (1-inch) pieces

1 Combine dressing and Worcestershire sauce in small bowl. Reserve 2 tablespoons dressing mixture. Combine beef, mushrooms and remaining dressing mixture in large resealable food storage bag. Seal bag; turn to coat. Marinate in refrigerator 30 to 60 minutes.

2 For sauce, combine mayonnaise, sour cream, garlic, rosemary and salt in small bowl. Cover and refrigerate until ready to use.

3 Prepare grill for direct cooking. Thread beef, mushrooms, zucchini and bell pepper alternately onto 8 (10-inch) skewers. Discard remaining marinade.

4 Grill skewers over medium-high heat 6 to 8 minutes or until desired doneness, turning occasionally. Brush with reserved 2 tablespoons dressing mixture before serving. Serve with sauce.

MAKES 4 SERVINGS

FIRE & SPICE

Grilled Picante BBQ Chicken

¾ cup PACE® Picante Sauce
¼ cup barbecue sauce
6 skinless, boneless chicken breast halves (about 1½ pounds)

1 Stir the picante sauce and barbecue sauce in a small bowl. Reserve all but ½ cup picante sauce mixture to serve with the chicken.

2 Lightly oil the grill rack and heat the grill to medium. Grill the chicken for 15 minutes or until cooked through, turning and brushing often with the remaining picante sauce mixture. Discard the remaining picante sauce mixture.

3 Serve the chicken with the reserved picante sauce mixture.

MAKES 6 SERVINGS

Kitchen Tip: This simple basting sauce also makes a zesty dipping sauce for chicken wings or nuggets.

Prep Time: 5 minutes
Cook Time: 15 minutes
Total Time: 20 minutes

Chipotle-Rubbed Flank Steak

1 packet (1.25 ounces) ORTEGA® Chipotle Taco Seasoning Mix, divided

½ cup water

¼ cup REGINA® Red Wine Vinegar

1½ to 2 pounds flank steak

1 tablespoon olive oil

1 small onion, diced

1 tablespoon ORTEGA® Fire-Roasted Diced Green Chiles

1 cup ORTEGA® Garden Salsa

Juice from ½ lime

COMBINE one half of seasoning mix, water and vinegar in shallow dish. Add steak and turn to coat well. Marinate 15 minutes in refrigerator. Turn over and marinate 15 minutes longer.

HEAT oil in small saucepan over medium heat. Add onion; cook and stir 5 minutes or until translucent. Stir in chiles and salsa; cook and stir over low heat 5 minutes.

SPRINKLE remaining seasoning mix over both sides of steak. Broil or grill steak over high heat 5 minutes on each side, or to desired doneness. Let stand 5 minutes before slicing against grain. To serve, drizzle with sauce and lime juice.

MAKES 4 TO 6 SERVINGS

Tip: For a less formal meal, create flavorful tacos instead. Simply serve the steak and sauce in soft tortillas, and garnish with shredded lettuce, diced tomatoes and shredded cheese, if desired.

Spicy Grilled Quesadillas

8 (8-inch) flour tortillas
8 ounces shredded Cheddar cheese (about 2 cups)
1 jar (16 ounces) PACE® Picante Sauce
1 cup diced cooked chicken
4 medium green onions, chopped (about ½ cup)
   Vegetable oil
1 container (8 ounces) sour cream

1 Top each of 4 tortillas with ½ cup cheese, ¼ cup picante sauce, ¼ cup chicken and 2 tablespoons green onions. Brush the edges of the tortillas with water. Top with the remaining tortillas and press the edges to seal.

2 Lightly oil the grill rack and heat the grill to medium. Brush the tops of the quesadillas with oil. Place the quesadillas oil-side down on the grill rack. Brush the other side of the quesadillas with oil. Grill the quesadillas for 5 minutes or until the cheese is melted, turning the quesadillas over once during grilling. Remove the quesadillas from the grill and let them stand for 2 minutes.

3 Cut each quesadilla into 4 wedges. Serve with the remaining picante sauce and sour cream.

MAKES 4 SERVINGS

Kitchen Tip: Quesadillas are an easy way to turn leftover meat and shredded cheese into a whole new meal. You can even combine different varieties of shredded cheese to make the 2 cups needed in this recipe.

Serving Suggestion: Serve with Spanish-style rice and fresh carrot sticks. For dessert, serve fresh apple slices with prepared caramel sauce.

Prep Time: 10 minutes
Grill Time: 7 minutes
Total Time: 17 minutes

FIRE & SPICE

Szechuan Tuna Steaks

    4 tuna steaks (6 ounces each), cut 1 inch thick
    ¼ cup dry sherry or sake
    ¼ cup soy sauce
    1 tablespoon dark sesame oil
    1 teaspoon hot chili oil *or* **¼ teaspoon red pepper flakes**
    1 clove garlic, minced
    3 tablespoons chopped fresh cilantro

1 Place tuna in single layer in large shallow glass dish. Combine sherry, soy sauce, sesame oil, hot chili oil and garlic in small bowl. Reserve ¼ cup soy sauce mixture at room temperature. Pour remaining soy sauce mixture over tuna. Cover and marinate in refrigerator 40 minutes, turning once.

2 Prepare grill for direct grilling. Oil grid.

3 Drain tuna, discarding marinade. Grill tuna over medium-high heat 6 minutes or until seared but still slightly soft in center,* turning halfway through grilling time.

4 Transfer tuna to cutting board; cut into thin slices. Drizzle with reserved soy sauce mixture; sprinkle with cilantro.

MAKES 4 SERVINGS

Tuna becomes dry and tough if overcooked. Cook to medium doneness for best results.

FIRE & SPICE

Spicy Hunan Ribs

1⅓ cups hoisin sauce or CATTLEMEN'S® Golden Honey Barbecue
    Sauce

⅔ cup FRANK'S® REDHOT® XTRA Hot Cayenne Pepper Sauce
    or FRANK'S® REDHOT® Original Cayenne Pepper Sauce

¼ cup soy sauce

2 tablespoons brown sugar

2 tablespoons dark sesame oil

2 tablespoons grated peeled ginger root

4 cloves garlic, crushed through a press

2 full racks pork spareribs, trimmed (about 6 pounds)

1 Combine hoisin sauce, XTRA Hot Sauce, soy sauce, brown sugar, sesame oil, ginger and garlic; mix well.

2 Place ribs in large resealable plastic food storage bags. Pour 1½ cups sauce mixture over ribs. Seal bags and marinate in refrigerator 1 to 3 hours or overnight.

3 Prepare grill for indirect cooking over medium-low heat (250°F). Place ribs on rib rack or in foil pan; discard marinade. Cook on covered grill 2½ to 3 hours until very tender. Baste with remaining sauce during last 15 minutes of cooking. If desired, grill ribs over direct heat at end of cooking to char slightly.

MAKES 4 TO 6 SERVINGS

Tip: Use Kansas City or St. Louis-style ribs for this recipe.

Prep Time: 5 minutes
Marinate Time: 1 hour
Cook Time: 3 hours

FIRE & SPICE

Honey Mustard Glazed Salmon with Tropical Fruit Salsa

   3 tablespoons spicy brown mustard
   2 tablespoons honey
   ¾ teaspoon salt, divided
   ¼ teaspoon hot pepper sauce
   1 can (15.25 ounces) DOLE® Tropical Fruit, drained and diced
   1 avocado, peeled and diced
   ⅓ cup diced red bell pepper
   ¼ cup chopped DOLE® Red Onion
   1 tablespoon lime juice
   1⅓ pounds salmon fillets

Stir together mustard, honey, ½ teaspoon salt and hot pepper sauce in small bowl.

Combine tropical fruit, avocado, bell pepper, onion, lime juice and remaining ¼ teaspoon salt. Cover; refrigerate salsa until ready to serve.

Grill or broil salmon 4 to 5 minutes, brushing with honey-mustard glaze; turn over. Grill or broil 4 to 5 minutes more or until desired doneness, brushing with remaining glaze. Serve salmon with tropical fruit salsa.

MAKES 4 SERVINGS

Prep Time: 20 minutes
Grill Time: 10 minutes

FIRE & SPICE

Grilled Chicken with Spicy Black Beans and Rice

        2 boneless skinless chicken breasts (about 4 ounces each)
        1 teaspoon Caribbean jerk seasoning
        1 teaspoon olive oil
      ½ cup finely diced green bell pepper
        2 tablespoons chopped onion
        1 tablespoon chipotle chili powder
    1½ cups hot cooked rice
        1 cup rinsed and drained canned black beans
        3 tablespoons diced pimiento
        2 tablespoons chopped pimiento-stuffed green olives
        2 tablespoons chopped fresh cilantro (optional)
           Lime wedges (optional)

1 Prepare grill for direct cooking. Oil grid.

2 Rub chicken with jerk seasoning. Grill chicken over medium heat 8 to 10 minutes or until no longer pink in center, turning once.

3 Meanwhile, heat oil in medium saucepan or skillet over medium heat. Add bell pepper, onion and chili powder; cook and stir until vegetables are tender.

4 Add rice, beans, pimiento and olives to saucepan; cook and stir about 3 minutes or until heated through.

5 Slice chicken; serve with rice mixture. Sprinkle with cilantro, if desired. Garnish with lime wedges.

MAKES 2 SERVINGS

Grilled Swordfish with Hot Red Sauce

    2 tablespoons Sesame Salt (recipe follows)
    4 swordfish or halibut steaks (about 1½ pounds total)
    ¼ cup chopped green onions
    2 tablespoons hot bean paste*
    2 tablespoons soy sauce
    4 teaspoons sugar
    4 cloves garlic, minced
    1 tablespoon dark sesame oil
    ⅛ teaspoon black pepper

Available in specialty stores or Asian markets.

1 Prepare Sesame Salt.

2 Rinse swordfish and pat dry with paper towels. Place in shallow dish.

3 Combine green onions, 2 tablespoons Sesame Salt, hot bean paste, soy sauce, sugar, garlic, sesame oil and pepper in small bowl; mix well.

4 Spread mixture over both sides of fish; cover with plastic wrap. Marinate in refrigerator 30 minutes.

5 Prepare grill for direct cooking. Oil grid.

6 Remove fish from marinade; discard remaining marinade. Grill fish over medium-high heat 8 to 10 minutes or until fish is opaque, turning once.

MAKES 4 SERVINGS

Sesame Salt: Heat small skillet over medium heat. Add ¼ cup sesame seeds; cook and stir about 3 minutes or until seeds are golden. Cool. Crush toasted sesame seeds and 1 teaspoon coarse salt with mortar and pestle or process in clean spice grinder. Store in refrigerator.

FIRE & SPICE

Chipotle-Lime Grilled Cornish Hens

4 TYSON® Cornish Game Hens, thawed
1 tablespoon cumin seeds, crushed
2 teaspoons dried oregano
1 teaspoon olive or vegetable oil
4 garlic cloves, minced
2 teaspoons kosher (coarse) salt
4 teaspoons grated lime peel
½ cup lime juice
¼ cup olive oil
2 large canned chipotle chilies in adobo sauce, finely chopped,
**   with 1 teaspoon adobo sauce**
**   Salt and black pepper, to taste**

1 Heat small skillet over medium heat. Add cumin seeds; heat 1 minute. Add oregano; cook and stir 30 seconds or until cumin is lightly toasted. Add 1 teaspoon oil and garlic; cook 30 seconds. Remove from heat.

2 Blend cumin mixture and remaining ingredients, except hens, in small bowl. Rinse hens with cold water and pat dry with paper towels. Lightly salt and pepper inside of hens. Secure wings to hens and tie legs together with string, if desired. Place marinade in large plastic food storage bag; add hens and seal bag. Turn bag to coat hens evenly with marinade. Refrigerate at least 8 hours or overnight, turning occasionally.

3 Set up grill for indirect cooking: For gas grill, preheat all burners on high Turn one burner off; place food over "off" burner. Reset remaining burner(s) to medium. Close lid. For charcoal grill, arrange hot coals around outer edge of grill. Place disposable pan in open space; place food over open area. Close lid. Heat to medium.

4 Remove hens from marinade; discard leftover marinade. Place hens hens (not touching) over indirect heat on grill. Grill hens, covered, 50 to 60 minutes or until done (internal temp 180°F). Let stand 5 minutes before serving.

MAKES 4 SERVINGS

Jerk-Spiced Beef Sirloin

2 cups SWANSON® Beef Stock
¼ cup olive oil
3 tablespoons Jamaican jerk seasoning
2 tablespoons balsamic vinegar
3 cloves garlic, minced
1 boneless beef top loin or beef sirloin steak, 2 inches thick (about 3 pounds)
1 tablespoon lemon juice
1 tablespoon chopped fresh cilantro leaves

1 Stir the stock, oil, seasoning, vinegar and garlic in a shallow, nonmetallic dish or gallon-size resealable plastic bag. Add the steak and turn to coat. Cover the dish or seal the bag and refrigerate for 8 hours, turning the steak over a few times during marinating.

2 Lightly oil the grill rack and heat the grill to medium. Remove the steak from the marinade and pour the marinade in a 1-quart saucepan.

3 Heat the marinade over medium-high heat to a boil. Reduce the heat to low. Cook for 10 minutes. Stir in the lemon juice and cilantro. Keep warm.

4 Grill the steak for 28 minutes for medium-rare or to desired doneness, turning once during grilling. Slice the steak and serve with the lemon-cilantro sauce.

MAKES 12 SERVINGS

Kitchen Tip: Marinate the steak and refrigerate for up to 24 hours. When ready to serve, prepare as directed above.

Pollo Diavolo (Deviled Chicken)

8 skinless bone-in chicken thighs (2½ to 3 pounds)
¼ cup olive oil
3 tablespoons lemon juice
6 cloves garlic, minced
1 to 2 teaspoons red pepper flakes
3 tablespoons butter, softened
1 teaspoon dried or rubbed sage
1 teaspoon dried thyme
¾ teaspoon coarse salt
¼ teaspoon ground red pepper or black pepper
   Lemon wedges

1 Place chicken in large resealable food storage bag. Combine oil, lemon juice, garlic and red pepper flakes in small bowl. Pour mixture over chicken. Seal bag; turn to coat. Refrigerate at least 1 hour or up to 8 hours, turning once.

2 Prepare grill for direct cooking. Drain chicken; reserve marinade.

3 Place chicken on grid; brush with reserved marinade. Grill chicken, covered, over medium-high heat 8 minutes. Turn chicken; brush with remaining marinade. Grill, covered, 8 to 10 minutes or until cooked through (165°F).

4 Meanwhile, combine butter, sage, thyme, salt and ground red pepper in small bowl; mix well. Transfer chicken to serving platter; spread herb butter over chicken. Serve with lemon wedges.

MAKES 4 TO 6 SERVINGS

FIRE & SPICE

Zesty Steak Fajitas

¾ cup FRENCH'S® Worcestershire Sauce, divided
1 pound boneless top round, sirloin or flank steak
3 tablespoons taco seasoning mix
2 red or green bell peppers, cut into quarters
1 to 2 large onions, cut into thick slices
¾ cup chili sauce
8 (8-inch) flour or corn tortillas, heated
  Sour cream and shredded cheese (optional)

1 Pour ½ cup Worcestershire over steak in deep dish. Cover and refrigerate 30 minutes or up to 3 hours. Drain meat and rub both sides with seasoning mix. Discard marinade.

2 Grill meat and vegetables over medium-hot coals 10 to 15 minutes until meat is medium-rare and vegetables are charred, but tender.

3 Thinly slice meat and vegetables. Place in large bowl. Add chili sauce and remaining ¼ cup Worcestershire. Toss to coat. Serve in tortillas and garnish with sour cream and cheese.

MAKES 4 SERVINGS

Prep Time: 5 minutes
Cook Time: 15 minutes
Marinate Time: 30 minutes

VEGGIE OUT

Spicy Grilled Corn

- 2 tablespoons butter, softened
- 1 tablespoon chopped fresh parsley
- 2 teaspoons lemon juice
- ½ teaspoon salt
- ½ teaspoon black pepper
- ½ teaspoon red pepper flakes
- 4 ears corn, husks and silks removed

1 Prepare grill for direct cooking.

2 Combine butter, parsley, lemon juice, salt, black pepper and red pepper flakes in small bowl. Brush mixture evenly over corn.

3 Place two sheets of foil (about 12×18 inches each) on work surface; center 2 ears of corn on each piece of foil. Bring up sides of foil; fold over top and edges to seal packets.

4 Grill packets, covered, over medium-high heat about 15 minutes or until corn is tender, turning once.

MAKES 4 SERVINGS

Grilled Mesquite Vegetables

2 to 3 tablespoons MRS. DASH® Mesquite Grilling Blend
2 tablespoons olive oil, divided
1 eggplant, trimmed and cut into ½-inch slices
1 zucchini, quartered lengthwise
1 red onion, peeled and halved
2 red bell peppers, cut into large slices
2 green bell peppers, cut into large slices
1 tablespoon balsamic vinegar

Preheat barbecue grill to medium. In large bowl, combine Mrs. Dash® Mesquite Grilling Blend and 1 tablespoon olive oil. Add vegetables and toss until well coated. Place vegetables on grill. Cover and cook, turning vegetables once during cooking, until vegetables are tender and develop grill marks, about 3 to 4 minutes on each side. Remove vegetables from grill as soon as they are cooked. Coarsely chop vegetables into ½-inch pieces. Mix remaining olive oil and balsamic vinegar in large bowl. Add cut vegetables and toss to coat. Serve at room temperature.

MAKES 6 SERVINGS

Note: Grilling vegetables dehydrates them slightly and intensifies the flavors, while Mrs. Dash® Mesquite Grilling Blend adds a third dimension of flavor. This dish makes a colorful accompaniment to any grilled meat.

Prep Time: 10 minutes
Cook Time: 8 minutes

Pasta and Grilled Vegetable Salad with Cilantro Dressing

DRESSING

- 1 can (4 ounces) ORTEGA® Fire-Roasted Diced Green Chiles
- ¼ cup chopped fresh cilantro
- ¼ cup olive oil
- 1 tablespoon REGINA® Red Wine Vinegar
- ½ teaspoon POLANER® Minced Garlic
- Salt and black pepper, to taste

SALAD

- 1 red bell pepper, cored, seeded, cut in half
- 1 green bell pepper, cored, seeded, cut in half
- 1 medium zucchini, cut lengthwise into thin slices
- 1 medium yellow squash, cut lengthwise into thin slices
- 1 large red onion, cut into ½-inch-thick wedges
- 1 pound pasta shells or penne, cooked
- 1 jar (16 ounces) ORTEGA® Garden Vegetable Salsa
- ¼ cup firmly packed fresh basil, cut into thin strips
- Lettuce leaves (optional)

COMBINE chiles, cilantro, oil, vinegar and garlic in small bowl. Whisk until well blended. Season with salt and pepper, to taste. Set aside.

PREHEAT grill to medium-high heat, about 15 minutes. Lightly brush grill grid with vegetable oil.

GRILL bell peppers, zucchini, squash and onion 3 to 5 minutes per side or until fork-tender. Remove vegetables from grill; cut into bite-size pieces.

TOSS cooked pasta, salsa, grilled vegetables and basil in large bowl or on serving platter. Serve with dressing on lettuce leaves, if desired.

MAKES 6 TO 8 SERVINGS

VEGGIE OUT

Grilled Veggies and Couscous

⅓ cup pine nuts

1½ cups vegetable broth or water

1 tablespoon olive oil, plus additional oil for basting vegetables

½ teaspoon salt

1 cup uncooked couscous

1 medium zucchini, cut lengthwise into ½-inch slices

1 medium red bell pepper, cut in half

½ small red onion, sliced

¼ cup crumbled feta or basil-tomato flavored feta cheese

1 clove garlic, minced

   Salt and black pepper

½ teaspoon lemon pepper

1 Toast pine nuts in small nonstick skillet over medium heat 5 minutes or until light brown and fragrant. Set aside to cool.

2 Bring broth, 1 tablespoon oil and ½ teaspoon salt to a boil in small saucepan over medium-high heat. Stir in couscous. Remove from heat; cover and set aside.

3 Prepare grill for direct cooking.

4 Brush vegetables with olive oil. Grill zucchini and onion over medium-high heat 3 to 5 minutes until tender. Grill bell pepper 7 to 10 minutes or until skin is blackened. Place pepper in small plastic bag; seal and set aside 3 to 5 minutes. Remove from bag; peel off blackened skin. Chop vegetables.

5 Spoon couscous into serving bowl; fluff with fork. Add vegetables, pine nuts, cheese, garlic, salt and black pepper; mix well. Sprinkle with lemon pepper.

MAKES 4 TO 6 SERVINGS

  VEGGIE OUT

Teriyaki Tempeh with Pineapple

- 1 package (8 ounces) unseasoned soy tempeh
- 1 cup pineapple teriyaki sauce, plus additional for serving
- 1 cup uncooked rice
- ½ cup matchstick-size carrots
- ½ cup snow peas
- ½ cup matchstick-size red bell pepper strips
- 4 fresh pineapple rings

1 Heat 1 cup water in large deep skillet over high heat. Cut tempeh in half crosswise; add to skillet. Bring to a boil; reduce heat and simmer 10 minutes. Drain water; add 1 cup teriyaki sauce to tempeh in skillet. Bring to a simmer over medium heat; simmer 10 minutes, turning occasionally. Drain and reserve teriyaki sauce; add additional sauce, if necessary, to make ½ cup.

2 Meanwhile, cook rice according to package directions. Heat reserved teriyaki sauce in wok or large nonstick skillet over medium-high heat. Add carrots, snow peas and bell pepper; cook and stir 4 to 6 minutes or until crisp-tender. Add rice; stir to combine. Add additional teriyaki sauce, if desired.

3 Prepare grill for direct cooking.

4 Grill tempeh and pineapple over medium-high heat 10 minutes, turning once. Cut tempeh in half; serve with rice and pineapple.

MAKES 4 SERVINGS

Island Tempeh Sandwiches: Omit rice and vegetables. Serve tempeh and pineapple on soft rolls with arugula, additional teriyaki sauce and mayonnaise, if desired.

Portobello Mushroom Burger with Mozzarella

⅓ cup olive oil, plus more as needed

2 tablespoons chopped fresh parsley

2 teaspoons red wine vinegar

2 cloves garlic, minced

Salt and black pepper

4 large portobello mushrooms, stems trimmed

4 slices mozzarella cheese

4 thick slices red onion

4 kaiser or rustic rolls, split

2 cups DOLE® Leafy Romaine

4 tablespoons light mayonnaise or other favorite condiment

Mix oil, parsley, vinegar and garlic in shallow dish; season with salt and pepper. Add mushrooms and turn to coat thoroughly.

Grill mushrooms over medium-high heat, turning often, until just cooked through, 7 to 10 minutes; top with mozzarella and cook 2 minutes more. Lightly brush onion slices with olive oil or any remaining marinade and grill, turning once, about 5 minutes. Toast the rolls, cut side down, on grill.

Place one mushroom on bottom of each roll. Top each with grilled onion and romaine. Spread mayonnaise on cut side of roll tops and place on burgers. Serve with vegetable chips.

MAKES 4 SERVINGS

VEGGIE OUT

Grilled Vegetable Pizzas

    2 tablespoons olive oil
    1 clove garlic, minced
    1 red bell pepper, cut into quarters
    4 slices red onion, cut ¼ inch thick
    1 medium zucchini, halved lengthwise
    1 medium yellow squash, halved lengthwise
    1 cup prepared pizza sauce
  ¼ teaspoon red pepper flakes
    2 (10-inch) prepared pizza crusts
    2 cups (8 ounces) shredded fontinella or mozzarella cheese
  ¼ cup sliced fresh basil leaves

1 Prepare grill for direct cooking.

2 Combine 2 tablespoons oil and garlic in small bowl; brush over bell pepper, onion, zucchini and squash. Grill vegetables, covered, over medium heat 10 minutes or until crisp-tender, turning halfway through grilling time. Remove vegetables from grill.

3 Cut bell pepper lengthwise into ¼-inch strips. Cut zucchini and squash crosswise into ¼-inch slices. Separate onion slices into rings.

4 Combine pizza sauce and red pepper flakes in small bowl. Top crusts with pizza sauce mixture, cheese and grilled vegetables.

5 Grill pizzas, covered, over medium-low heat 5 to 6 minutes or until cheese is melted and crust is hot. Sprinkle with basil; cut into wedges. Serve warm.

MAKES 4 SERVINGS

Barbecue Seitan Skewers

1 package (8 ounces) cubed seitan
½ cup barbecue sauce, divided
1 red bell pepper, cut into 12 pieces
1 green bell pepper, cut into 12 pieces
12 mushrooms
1 zucchini, cut into 12 pieces

1 Separate seitan into cubes; place in medium bowl. Add ¼ cup barbecue sauce; stir to coat. Marinate in refrigerator 30 minutes. Soak four bamboo skewers in water 20 minutes.

2 Prepare grill for direct cooking. Oil grid. Thread seitan, bell peppers, mushrooms and zucchini onto skewers. Grill skewers, covered, over medium-high heat 8 minutes or until seitan is hot and glazed with sauce, brushing with some of remaining sauce and turning occasionally.

MAKES 4 SERVINGS

Szechuan Grilled Mushrooms

1 pound large mushrooms
2 tablespoons soy sauce
2 teaspoons peanut or vegetable oil
1 teaspoon dark sesame oil
1 clove garlic, minced
½ teaspoon crushed Szechuan peppercorns or red pepper flakes

1 Place mushrooms in large resealable food storage bag. Combine remaining ingredients in small bowl; pour over mushrooms. Seal bag; turn to coat. Marinate at room temperature 15 minutes.

2 Thread mushrooms onto skewers. Grill 10 minutes or until lightly browned, turning once. Serve immediately.

MAKES 4 SERVINGS

VEGGIE OUT

Grilled Pizza Margherita with Beer-Risen Crust

    ¾ cup beer
    1 package (¼ ounce) active dry yeast
    2 tablespoons plus 2 teaspoons extra virgin olive oil, divided
    1¾ to 2½ cups all-purpose flour
    1 teaspoon salt
    1½ pints grape tomatoes, halved
    1 clove garlic, minced
    ¼ teaspoon dried basil
    ⅛ teaspoon salt
    ⅛ teaspoon red pepper flakes
    6 ounces fresh mozzarella, cut into 12 slices
    10 fresh basil leaves, thinly sliced

1 Microwave beer in small microwavable bowl on HIGH 25 seconds. Stir in yeast and 2 teaspoons oil; let stand 5 minutes or until foamy. Combine 1¾ cups flour and salt in medium bowl. Add beer mixture; stir until dough pulls away from side of bowl. Turn dough out onto floured surface; knead 6 to 7 minutes or until smooth and elastic, adding enough additional flour to make smooth and elastic dough. Divide dough in half and form into balls. Dust with flour; place in separate medium bowls. Cover and let rise in warm, draft-free place about 1½ hours or until doubled in bulk.

2 Prepare grill for direct cooking over high heat. Oil grid.

3 Working with one ball at a time, turn dough onto lightly floured surface. Gently stretch dough to 9-inch round; transfer to floured baking sheets. Brush top of each round with half of remaining oil. Cover and let stand 10 minutes.

4 Meanwhile, heat 1 tablespoon oil in medium nonstick skillet over medium-high heat. Add tomatoes, garlic, dried basil, salt and red pepper flakes; cook 3 to 4 minutes or until tomatoes are very soft, stirring occasionally. Remove from heat

5 Reduce grill to medium heat. Carefully flip dough rounds onto grid, oiled side down. Grill, uncovered, 3 minutes or until bottoms are golden and well marked. Turn crusts; spread each with half of tomato mixture, leaving ½-inch border. Top with cheese; cover and grill 3 minutes or until cheese is melted and crusts are golden brown. Transfer to cutting board; sprinkle with basil and cut into 6 wedges. Serve immediately.

MAKES 4 SERVINGS

Acknowledgments

The publisher would like to thank the companies and organizations listed below for the use of their recipes and photographs in this publication.

The Beef Checkoff

Campbell Soup Company

Dole Food Company, Inc.

Mrs. Dash® is a registered trademark of B&G Foods, Inc.

National Turkey Federation

Ortega®, A Division of B&G Foods, Inc.

Reckitt Benckiser LLC.

Tyson Foods, Inc.

Unilever

INDEX **125**

Metric Conversion Chart

VOLUME MEASUREMENTS (dry)

1/8 teaspoon = 0.5 mL
1/4 teaspoon = 1 mL
1/2 teaspoon = 2 mL
3/4 teaspoon = 4 mL
1 teaspoon = 5 mL
1 tablespoon = 15 mL
2 tablespoons = 30 mL
1/4 cup = 60 mL
1/3 cup = 75 mL
1/2 cup = 125 mL
2/3 cup = 150 mL
3/4 cup = 175 mL
1 cup = 250 mL
2 cups = 1 pint = 500 mL
3 cups = 750 mL
4 cups = 1 quart = 1 L

VOLUME MEASUREMENTS (fluid)

1 fluid ounce (2 tablespoons) = 30 mL
4 fluid ounces (1/2 cup) = 125 mL
8 fluid ounces (1 cup) = 250 mL
12 fluid ounces (1 1/2 cups) = 375 mL
16 fluid ounces (2 cups) = 500 mL

WEIGHTS (mass)

1/2 ounce = 15 g
1 ounce = 30 g
3 ounces = 90 g
4 ounces = 120 g
8 ounces = 225 g
10 ounces = 285 g
12 ounces = 360 g
16 ounces = 1 pound = 450 g

DIMENSIONS

1/16 inch = 2 mm
1/8 inch = 3 mm
1/4 inch = 6 mm
1/2 inch = 1.5 cm
3/4 inch = 2 cm
1 inch = 2.5 cm

OVEN TEMPERATURES

250°F = 120°C
275°F = 140°C
300°F = 150°C
325°F = 160°C
350°F = 180°C
375°F = 190°C
400°F = 200°C
425°F = 220°C
450°F = 230°C

BAKING PAN SIZES

Utensil	Size in Inches/Quarts	Metric Volume	Size in Centimeters
Baking or Cake Pan (square or rectangular)	8×8×2	2 L	20×20×5
	9×9×2	2.5 L	23×23×5
	12×8×2	3 L	30×20×5
	13×9×2	3.5 L	33×23×5
Loaf Pan	8×4×3	1.5 L	20×10×7
	9×5×3	2 L	23×13×7
Round Layer Cake Pan	8×1½	1.2 L	20×4
	9×1½	1.5 L	23×4
Pie Plate	8×1¼	750 mL	20×3
	9×1¼	1 L	23×3
Baking Dish or Casserole	1 quart	1 L	—
	1½ quart	1.5 L	—
	2 quart	2 L	—